Guion and Friends

A Coloring and Activity Book

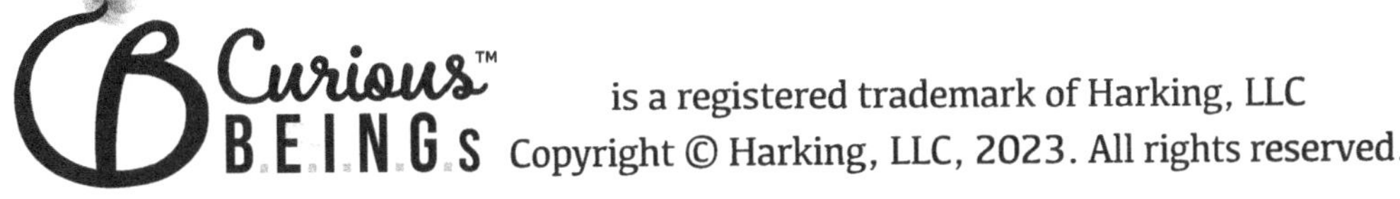

Guion and Rae
are best friends.

WORD SCRAMBLE
Unscramble the letters to spell out these words.

NORDAG

1. D _ _ _ _ G _

NOIL

2. _ _ _ O _

CAMIG

3. _ _ G _ _ _

GITHNK

4. K _ _ _ _ H _

SCALET

5. _ _ S _ _ _ E

MIGNODK

6. _ _ _ N _ _ _ D _ _ M

ANSWER ON PAGE 31.

Guion the Lion

WORD SEARCH

Search up, down, forwards and diagonally
for the words in the list. Circle the words as you find them.

V O P R K K W H D O
Z H J S U N R I S E
D G X M H I X D C S
R D I Q L G M B A Q
A L F R I H Z J S E
G I X C A T A N T O
O O L E J F L I L P
N N F R S E F V E M
G G J N R H V E B I
C Z T V B G B N P G

CASTLE
DRAGON
GIRAFFE

KNIGHT
LION
SUNRISE

GUION THE LION MAZE

Can you find your way from Guion's nose to the Ladybug?

ANSWER ON PAGE 31.

Guion imagines a magnificent castle.

Wilson the Giraffe

INTERLOCK PUZZLE

Use the letter clues to fill in the puzzle with the words from the list.

ANSWER ON PAGE 31.

Guion looks through the reed.

Rae isn't sure what she is supposed to see.

WORD SEARCH

Search up, down, forwards and diagonally
for the words in the list. Circle the words as you find them.

P N T T H Z U G S U
W G B R M E Z L H I
B A I P E U X F I J
M G T S I A E O P A
A E P E G R S U Y D
R L R L R I A U O U
C G B M Q J P T R A
E O S P A Y F W E E
S L K Q V I S G A W
O D N Z G A D L F X

GOLD
MERMAID
PIRATE

SHIP
TREASURE
WATER

MERMAID MAZE

Can you find your way from the turtle to the Starfish?

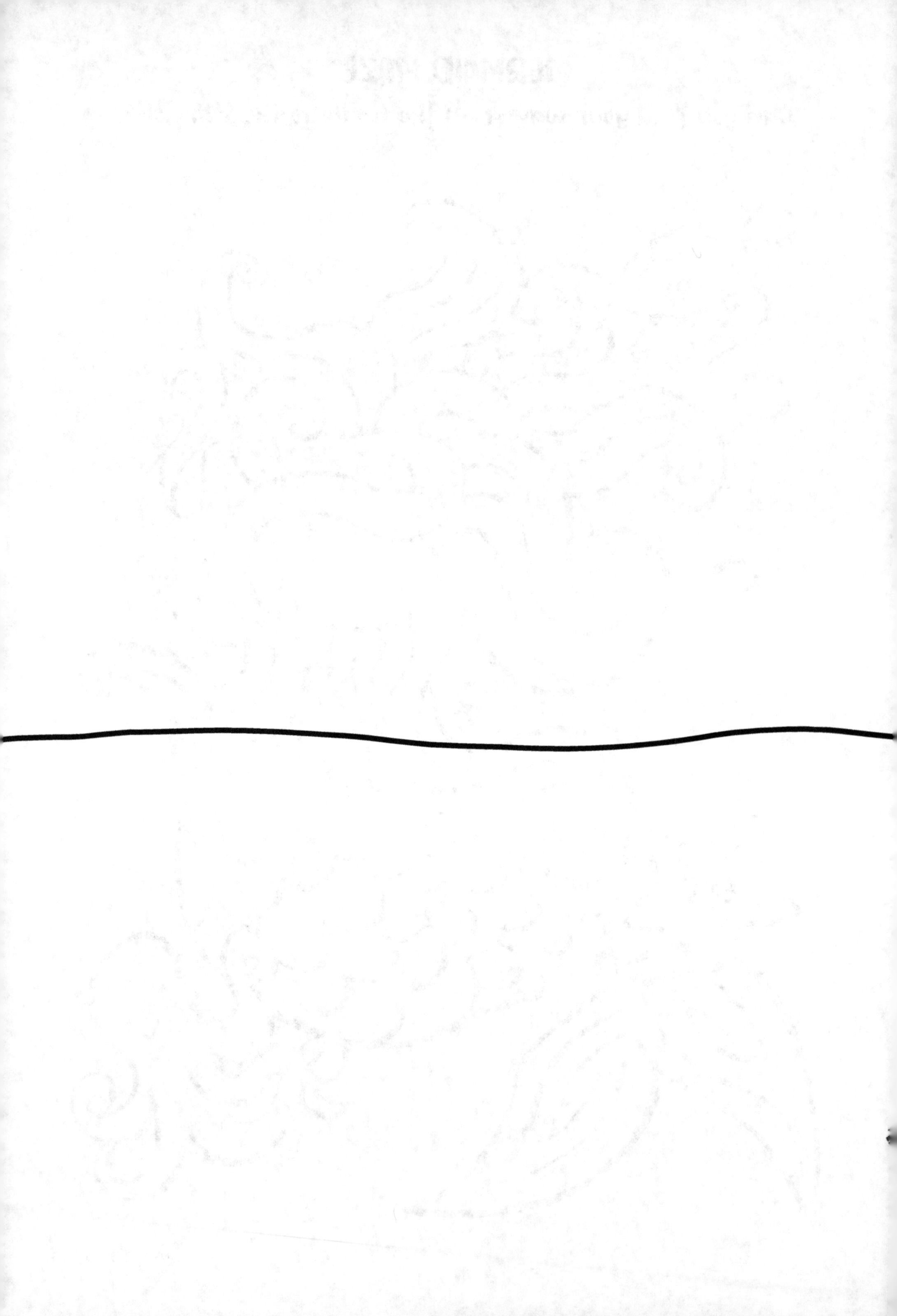

FINISH THE DRAWING

What does Hoke see floating on the water?
Is there anything below the surface?
Draw what you imagine!

Hoke the Hippo

TREASURE SUDOKU

Write in the letter for each missing picture. Remember, an image must appear only once in each row, column, and square grid.

SECRET CODE

Use the animal symbols to decode the secret message.

What is the name of the pirate ship
that Guion sees in the watering hole?

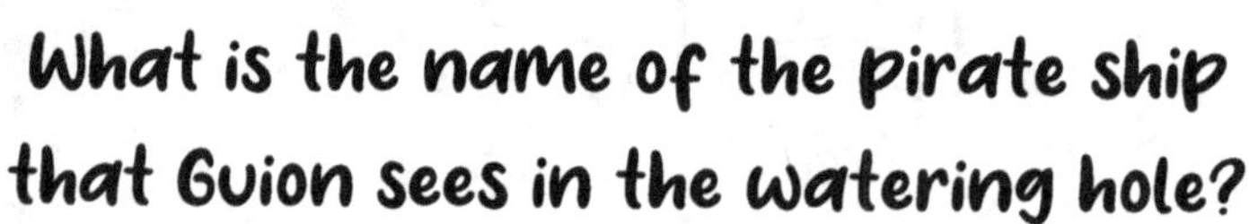

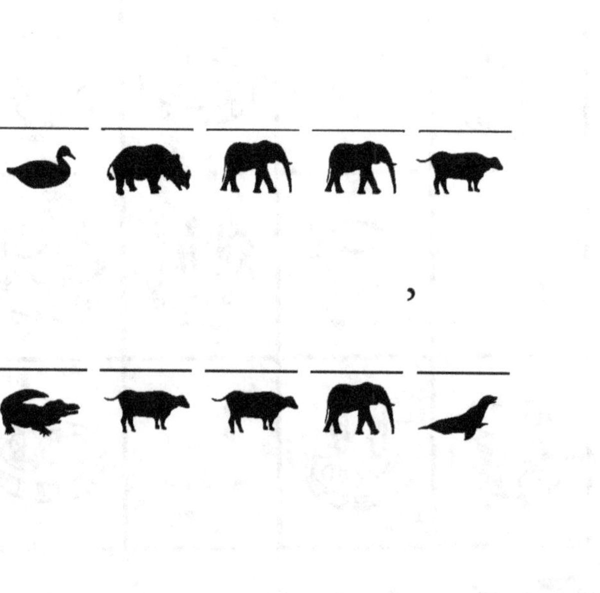

Olivia the Ostrich

The T-rex guards her nest.

WORD SEARCH

Search up, down, forwards and diagonally
for the words in the list. Circle the words as you find them.

X H J I E R I O M I
D D T M U N S S H W
V B I G W Q M T E K
L O N N U Y O R G B
D R L I O M K I G L
H T X C D S E C S W
A N O L A V A H T X
D N E Z D N A U T X
B B H S N E O D R M
N Z K Z T X T Q I Q

DINOSAUR	OSTRICH
EGGS	SMOKE
NEST	VOLCANO

T-rex

FOLLOW THE PATH

Follow the path to find each baby T-rex.
Write the letter next to each question.

WHICH LITTLE T-REX IS SITTING?

WHICH LITTLE T-REX IS HIDING?

WHICH LITTLE T-REX IS RUNNING?

ANSWER ON PAGE 31.

COLORING AND COUNTING

Color the footprints of Guion the Lion purple,
Wilson the Giraffe orange, and the T-rex green.

Count how many
of each footprint.

GUION ☐

WILSON ☐

T-REX ☐

ANSWER ON PAGE 31.

The best days...

Are even better with friends.

CONNECT THE CONSTELLATIONS
Connect the stars by numbers and letters
to form Leo the Lion and Draco the Dragon.

ANSWER KEY

1. D R A G O N
2. L I O N
3. M A G I C
4. K N I G H T
5. C A S T L E
6. K I N G D O M
page 4

page 5

page 6

page 7

page 10

page 11

page 14

page 15

page 18

page 19

QUEEN
ANNE'S
REVENGE
page 20

page 21

page 24

page 25

Follow the Path
WHICH LITTLE T-REX IS SITTING? B
WHICH LITTLE T-REX IS HIDING? A
WHICH LITTLE T-REX IS RUNNING? C
page 26

Count how many
of each footprint.
GUION 17
WILSON 14
T-REX 9
page 27

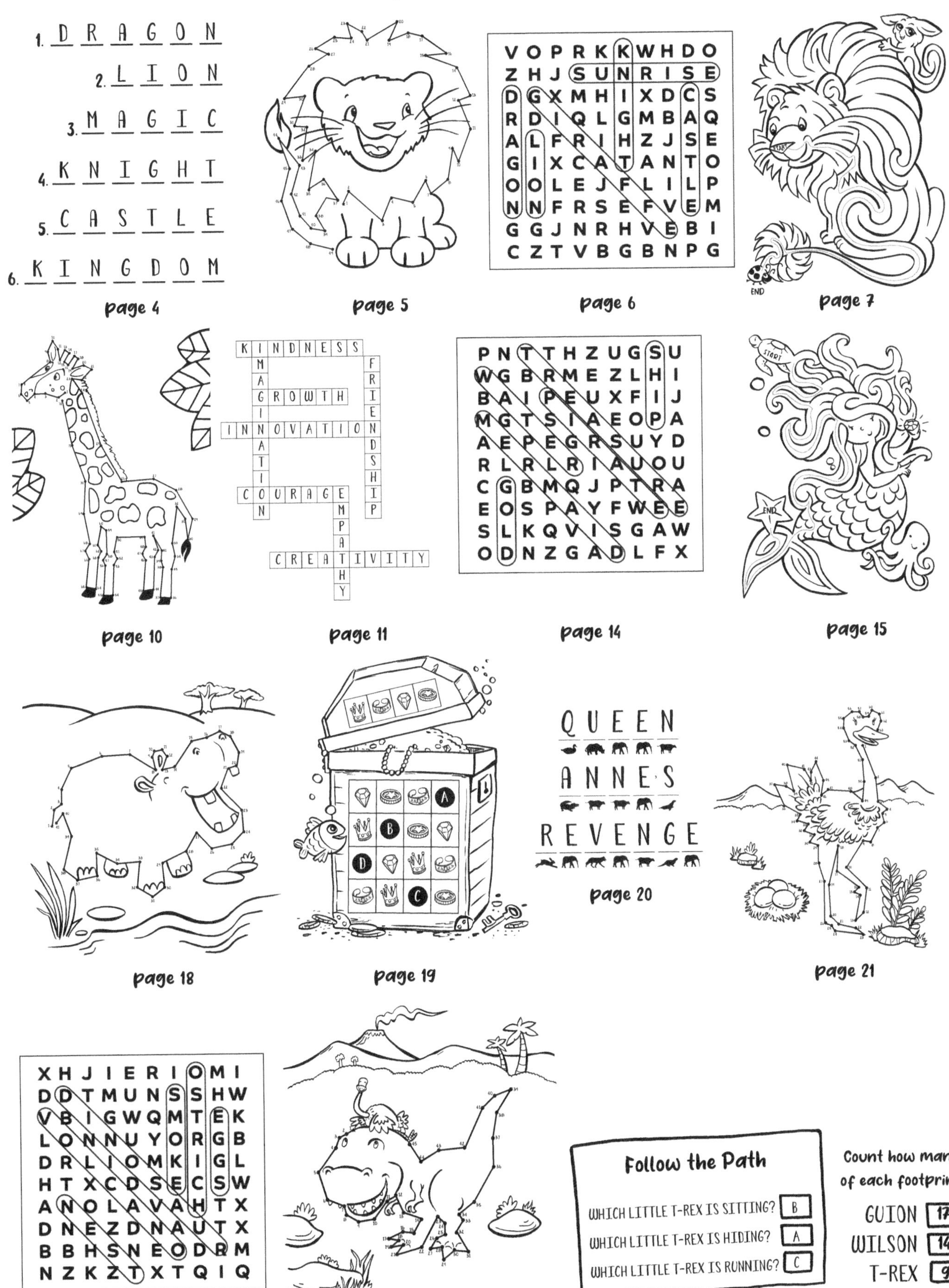

BLANK PAGE REQUESTED BY MANUFACTURER